Feed the Other Wolf

50 reflections on leadership

Inspired by popular, current telling
of teachings and lore attributed to
American Indigenous and Gullah peoples.

By

Timothy Hagler

Contact the author at: tim@thinkoutsideinsupplychain.com

Visit the author's healthcare supply chain and leadership blog at:

http://www.thinkoutsideinsupplychain.com/

Like us on Facebook:

https://www.facebook.com/TimHaglerSupplyChainIQ/

Forward

"Show respect for even the least of another living thing, and all things from the moon of the snow blowing like spirits upon the wind, to the moon of the popping trees, will be shown as respect for you." - Arapaho Proverb

Respect: Give it to get it!

The stories of the American indigenous people are as varied as the people themselves, and yet these tribal chronicles are consistently rooted in respect. Respect for all living things, respect for the vulnerability of life, respect for the struggle of daily accomplishment, and the intimate connections to all kinds of creatures, the earth, water, fire, and sky. The role of ancestry in these stories invites those who have come before us to join the narrative and advise our steps to make our way easier.

In this magnificent association with all that has come before us and all that remains forever, we have folklore and historical accounts, spiritual rituals and observations of the natural world, and vast libraries of teachings from our native ethnoecological heritage.

In this book, I will reach into a robust storeroom of familiar stories I have heard as a child growing up witnessing the Choctaw and Cherokee traditions of my father, and the Gullah culture from the islands and low country of South Carolina that as an adult, I have come to know and love as my home. From this deep well of ancestral context, I will bring to you, elements of an approach to leadership that has served as a light to my path since my first divisional directorship some time ago.

I am honored to share these stories and I hope that they will enlighten, encourage, teach, and even heal you as they have me, and generations of indigenous peoples before us.

Now, I will introduce you to the wolf that I have fed.

Two Wolves

An old Cherokee is teaching his son about life. "A great fight is going on inside of us my son," he said to the boy. "It is a violent and terrible quarrel between two wolves. One is evil – his name has been called Anger, Envy, Sorrow, Regret, Greed, Arrogance, Self-Pity, Guilt, Resentment, Lies, False Pride, Superiority, and Ego." He continued, "The name of the other wolf is good in nature and his name has been called Joy, Peace, Love, Hope, Serenity, Humility, Kindness, Benevolence, Empathy, Generosity, Truth, Compassion, and Faith. My son, this fight I am telling you about is going on inside of you... Just as it has inside of every other person as well."

The boy thought about it for a minute and then asked, "Father, do you know which wolf will win this fight?" "Yes, I do," said the boy's father. The boy follows with the inevitable question... "Which wolf will win?" The old Cherokee simply replied, "The one you feed."

In the context of contemporary leadership, feed the angry, evil wolf and you will only harvest pain and difficulty, even in times of great opportunity... Feed the good and kind wolf and you will reap opportunity even from times of pain and difficulty.

I was traveling along the beautiful Blue Ridge Parkway with my great friend Gene England and our wives for a weekend getaway on the Nantahala River in North Carolina. We had stopped for a few moments to take some scenic photographs and ended up giving in to the temptation to enjoy an echo or two by yelling short quips into the valley. Gene is a career military leader who retired with a prestigious rank and a tremendous store of gratitude and respect from those he had in his command during his service. I have often said that whatever Gene does not know about leadership isn't worth knowing. That day on the Blue Ridge Parkway, as our echoes rang back in a cacophonous chorus surrounding us in a wonderful swirl of sound, it didn't surprise me that Gene had a ready parable. "Tim, these echoes are your demonstration of leadership... You are getting back exactly what you sent out... multiplied."

My friends, if you are hearing echoes of unwelcome attitudes from your team, for heaven's sake, feed the other wolf.

"If uno de kno whey uno de gwine, den uno de kno whey uno de com fro." – *Gullah Proverb*

"To know where you are going you need to know where you came from"

Writer and editor, Rebecca Solnit said: "Sense of place is the sixth sense, an internal compass and map made by memory and special perception together." That is to say, that of all of our journeys, all of our goals, aspirations, intentions, it is Solnit's internal compass that gives us the "here" so we can point our way from this one place. It is the first rule of navigation – find out where you are.

As a leader, you are as responsible for the competent understanding of the current state as you are for the architecture of the desired future state.

Which leads me to the second rule of navigation…

"The important step in getting somewhere is deciding you are not going to stay where you are."
- Gullah Proverb

There is something to be said for the status quo... And that thing is 'goodbye.' Surround yourself by those who passionately challenge the status quo and you will never have to settle for anything less than excellence.

"Hear whispers, and there will be no screams." – Cherokee Proverb

I know a number of leaders who manage great cost and productivity improvement campaigns, based on precise data-driven reconnaissance, but they are not someone who steps forward assertively when it is time to take on a role of the decisive leader who studies fast and decides fast. Frankly, as leaders, we are often actively called on to take decisive action while a challenge is still a whisper and not let the situation escalate to a scream. To some this skill comes naturally, but for others, it feels to them like opening the refrigerator door abruptly but the little light just doesn't come on right away. If you believe that great decisive leaders are born and not made, think again... There are tactics that we can manage that will help our decision-making speed and confidence improve, as well as maneuvers that will slow that refrigerator door light to the point that we will catch a chill while waiting in the darkness.

The light seems to speed up when you can quickly "apply to the COWS for a decision." Nimbly list your **C**riteria and **O**ptions... apply **W**eight to the criteria, then **S**core the options, and pick the better result.

The light slows down when: you set the threshold for accuracy too high, you allow yourself too many choices or your perception of risk is too high for impromptu decisions.

When the light is off and the door is closed your unattended-to blind spots will ultimately slow your response time simply because you have set yourself traps by not communicating strategic direction to your likely collaborators or your team, not being clear about priorities, or if you have poorly communicated expectations to your team. But the real trap to slow you down is if you have delayed intervening and allowed poor performance for too long.

One more thought... I know it is counter-intuitive but if you only have two hours to cut firewood, sharpen your ax for the first hour.

- Take a deep breath and consider the future impact this decision could have.
- Even though the clock is ticking always take the time to gather as many data as you can.
- Allow some time to give credence to your instincts as well as your logic.
-

Being decisive with problems when they are small, will keep you from having to deal with long and invasive solutions campaigns to fix the same issues when they deteriorate into a state of crisis.

"As the serpent, the coyote, and your own footsteps; the life you live will be known by the tracks you leave behind." - Aphorism of the Dakota People

Dedicate yourself fully to the things that give your life significance and purpose.

Better yourself.

Don't be shy.

Connect.

Share what you know.

Be authentic.

Get to the root of the issue.

Invest in others.

Influence.

If someone is treated unfairly, take up their fight.

Allow your tide to rise... All boats will lift with you.

"Every stick and every stone upon the earth has a spiritual essence, all we see are manifestations of the Wakan Tanka (Great Mystery)." - Lakota Sioux Teaching

Micah, an 8th-century B.C. Hebrew prophet said it this way... "This is what is required of you: to act justly, to love faithfulness, and to walk humbly with your God." (Old Testament, Micah 6:8)

The phrase Wakan Tanka is the phrase that was commonly misinterpreted as "Great Spirit" when relating native proverbs and teachings. It actually describes the "Great Mystery" and, as such, it is not to be explained, it is a matter of respect for the holiness of creation that we understand that all things have essence and we should be humble as we confidently take our place in the Great Mystery.

Humble leaders are highly effective, and they generate a following that is near-apostolic.

The great power of a humble leader is in:

- Realizing people are to be judged by their own strengths not the strengths of their leader.
- Knowing that true leadership strength comes from sensing, focusing, and developing talent in others.
- Self-awareness, being reflective and spending adequate time in discernment.
- Gratitude.
- The expectation of excellence from themselves and others.

- Developing a safe space to challenge the status quo and for excellence to flourish.

"Dog taller sittin' stidduh stannin'..." (A dog is taller when it sits than when it stands.) - Traditional Gullah Adage

A leader can become so addicted to intensity that everything seems emergent and nothing truly stands out as uniquely important. This is highly confusing to those we are entrusted with leading and manufactures ambiguity where there would otherwise be organic clarity. An attitude on intensity that is always 'switched on' will block self-awareness and distort lucidity necessary to be able to effectively prioritize and respond to business and life challenges.

Don't go passive... practice alert watchfulness demonstrated by an open, calm, attentive presence.

The higher value a leader places on an attentive, relaxed attitude, the more benefit our teams will garner from knowing that they are being directed from a state of poised command, rather than the value-draining confusion of manic drive and misplaced intensity.

"Muh farruh in de murruh blonguh muh self."
(I see my father in my own reflection in the mirror) – Traditional Gullah Saying

The Gullah people were quite concerned with our ancestor's countenance in a reflective glass. When a community member passed away, Gullah communities would turn mirrors to the wall or cover them so the spirits would not be trapped in the reflection... Some Gullah communities held a belief that once trapped inside the mirror these spirits would watch over the lives of the community and advise those that looked at their reflections in the mirror.

Once I asked my father if he believed in ghosts, he said "Sure I do, just look in the mirror, son." Continuing, "your reflection holds the ghost of my father, and his father as well. Your image is a welcoming call for the spirit of our ancestors to live on and be part of our lives, and our children's lives."

To experience the power of ancestry and influence of those who are "advisors from the mirror" of the teams that we lead, try this... When a facilitating a small group, explain that we are an amalgam of ancestors and those who strongly influenced them, and from our own mirrors we reflect them in every interaction and decision. Ask each member of the team to tell the group about the ancestor or ancestral influencer that comes to mind at that moment. When you know the name of the person they "introduce" to the group, welcome that person to the room. (Example: "We welcome your mother to our discussion today and we are glad she is sharing her wisdom with us.") This exercise grounds the meeting participants in the present and gives them a safe environment to be genuine as well as quickly providing a robust base of understanding relative to the broader issues and people who that will ultimately prove to be influential to the individual team members participating that day.

"It does not require many words, to speak the truth." - Chief Joseph of the Nez Perce

The worst thing for a leader to do is to lie or even 'spin' the truth to their team. To lie is to demonstrate that the team is simply not worthy of the truth.

When being straight-forward is made difficult by bad news or something that will be hard for the team to hear, consider the following.

Think... You may want to pull the Band-Aid off quickly and get the initial hurt over with, but the message deserves you thinking through the time and place you deliver the news and the forum that you employ to deliver it. Be transparent and timely, but think it through to mitigate unintended consequences.

Brevity.

Clarity.

Empathy... This will include giving the team some space to think through the message and consider anything they need to have clarified, and what the impact is to them. And now - you will listen deeply to them.

Surprises are for birthdays, not your team... As a leader, you should have been communicating on team or even company performance and potential mitigation to missed targets, etc.

Be timely.

If you don't put it in writing, communication simply didn't happen.

You are going to have to address "why." You are a leader; you know "why" – be transparent.

It's worth saying again here... Don't spin. The facts are the facts.

Silver lining... While spin leads to false hope, the responsibility of leadership is to provide a level of solution or a basis for solution ideation to proceed. Be realistic, but show the team where new opportunities are indeed presenting themselves so they don't simply wander through the wilderness of bad news unled, and find themselves organizationally lost.

Season well with respect – dignity – follow-up and follow-through.

"Higher saa'puhn top de tree, de more he 'spose."
(The higher status an undesirable leader attains,
the more of their vulnerabilities are exposed as
well.) - Gullah Proverb

"The bigger they are, the harder they fall" is a worthwhile admonishment for all of us not to get too big for our britches, but it has a specific stinging, poignancy when it is applied to someone who is attaining artificially inflated status. The new vice president that was promoted on the accolades better shared with their team, but instead they took the credit... The political leader who was elected by running a slick (and expensive) campaign and now owes monumental favors to over-generous contributors... The man who has just "married well" into wealth and stature, but is hiding a secret second life including a humble wife and family in the suburbs.

As a leader, you have ample temptation to 'cut a few corners' with only quick status as an incremental reward. In doing so you have struck the Faustian bargain, and you will learn the high price to pay for this "crossroads" decision just as Robert Johnson in the bluesman-come-superstar legend. You could have taken a path that would raise the profile of the team with you, but instead you chose a path of derivative prestige that will ultimately leave you alone, exposed, ultimately knocked down a limb or two on the tree you are climbing, and your team publicly humiliated.

As the author Johnny Dent Jr., tells us "Be as advertised" ... and "The true definition of a phony is a high flyer with low mileage."

"You never really know your friends from your enemies until the ice breaks." - Native Alaskan Proverb

You are the boss, and as such, there, of course, needs to be clear interpersonal boundaries. The best times to be a friend to someone you work with are…

- When they cry…
  - Likely.
- When they need to share being happy with someone…
  - Could be, but boundaries still exist.
- If they need a hug…
  - A mental hug.
- When they need a shoulder…
  - It is still a business; it will be a quick turn-around effort.
- When they need a friend, but don't deserve one…
  - Probably better territory for Facebook.
- When their ice breaks.
  - Now! Life just gave you a battlefield promotion to 'friend.'

"Ku`ia ka hele a ka na`au ha`aha`a."
(Hesitant walks the humble hearted.) - Native
Hawaiian Saying

A humble leader will walk carefully, so her steps do not hurt others.

I don't think anyone ever aspires to leadership just so they can walk all over people, but I have observed that a great number of leaders are unaware of how constant intensity and throwing their organizational weight around can end up with the unintended outcomes of effectively rolling over the top of their teams.

"Dog got four feet but can't walk but one road." - Gullah saying, likely attributable to a Caribbean heritage proverb.

Why do we bother with visions of the future when today's problems are so immediate and overwhelming? Doesn't it feel more like we need problem-solving in the here and now? As a leader, if you only focus on putting out fires and solving immediate problems you lose out on great opportunities for your team to benefit from the generation of common goals, hopes, and encouragement that a clear forward-looking vision affords. Both problem-solving and visioning are important, but visioning gifts a team with a sense of control and something important to move toward, and is the hosts of creative thinking, passion, and innovation.

But visioning has a utility for the immediate environment as well... Vision keeps us on a single road with a clear destination. A strategic vision punctuates the team's journey with necessary way-finding signs to assure them that even in the most difficult times, mired in apparent ambiguity, they are still headed in the right direction, and success is indeed just ahead.

Have some fun with team visioning by conducting a "Merlin" exercise.

Dress up as a wizard (be creative, enjoy the moment) ... Magically transport the team ahead to an award ceremony celebrating their great success and the transformational contribution that is being held five years in the future. The team is being interviewed by a journalist from a prestigious industry magazine. Here are the questions...

- What is the most important work you did?
- What did it feel like to work on this team?
- What do you remember about the one thing that really got you started on the right path?
- What do you remember that your customers were concerned about five years ago as you were just getting started?
- What does senior management say about you now?
- What will you do to sustain the gains you have made?

"In our every deliberation, we must consider the impact of our decisions on the next seven generations." - From The Great Law of the Iroquois Confederacy

As leaders we can influence people and organizations by marshaling resources and support that will make life better for our communities, help where (without us) some people simply won't have the assets and influence to make a difference in their own condition, and of course - help sustain the planet. St Luke admonishes "... much is required of those entrusted with much." Luke 12:48.

How do you lead from a point of influence and drive decisions that consider generations of benefit from your community footprint? Think about these impacts.

Will your business enterprise help to solve real-life challenges for the communities that include your customers and employees?

Do you create job opportunities from people who have little chance of getting a job offer without your intervention?

Do you regularly allow your team to use their outstanding coordinated skill for the sake of a pro bono project? (example: a corporate marketing team that volunteers to conduct a campaign for a non-profit charity.)

Do you encourage managers to give employees paid time off to volunteer?

Do you donate a share of your gain to charity? (Idea: For teams that are support service and don't directly contribute revenue, you can still participate. If your team has favorable-to-budget expense performance, you can influence your company to let them choose a charity to donate half of the budget favorability to.)

I asked a Native Alaskan colleague for some Inuit wisdom, and he told me...

"Unless you are the lead sled dog, the scenery never changes." At the time I thought he was being funny for my benefit, but I have learned that this quote is attributable to author Bob Mitchley. But since a native Alaskan told it to me, and it has a ring of native wisdom, I am happy to include it in my portfolio of indigenous proverb.

The privilege of leadership is in leading, but it is not exactly cutting edge talent stewardship if you never give the rising stars on your team a chance to get out front and really feel the wind on their face as they set the pace and carve a path for their colleagues to follow. Authors Julie Gebauer and Don Lowman share in their book, *Closing the Engagement Gap*, a powerful algorithm for us to apply as we bring forward our up and coming superstars: 'Know them, grow them, inspire them, involve them, reward them.'

As you anticipate approaching key career 'moments that matter' consider an investment of your developing human capital on them instead of keeping all the "better scenery" for yourself.

"A hard head makes a soft behind." (Ignoring wise counsel is a bad idea.) - Gullah and Sea Island Creole Traditional Axiom

King Solomon said it this way... "Where there is no guidance, a people falls, but in an abundance of counselors there is safety." Proverbs 11:14

How do you go about asking for advice?

- What are your thoughts on ...? (be specific)
- Can you give me feedback and tips on ...?
- Can you help me with ...?
- Thank you!

This process is challenging, but I think you can see that the best among us will master the approach in no time at all. Or you can just 'Google it.'

"Take nothing but memories, leave nothing but footprints!" — Chief Seattle

Overconsumption is a situation where resource use has outpaced the sustainable capacity of the ecosystem. A prolonged pattern of overconsumption leads to environmental degradation and the eventual loss of resource bases.

Just as it is in our concern to sustain our natural resources, it is paralleled in how we often overconsume our available human resources as well. How do you know that you are overconsuming and burning out your team?

The workplace attitude changes.

The team avoids you.

Absenteeism increases.

Employees start hoarding vacation days and working longer hours.

Team members that are normally averse to confrontation begin pushing back on new task assignments.

Team turnover picks up.

If you conclude that you are over working team and overconsuming success-critical skills, what do you do to reverse the effect?

First TURN OFF THE FIRE HOSE BOSS! Then prioritize, balance, recognize, reward, and as Jimmy Buffet wrote, "breath in – breath out – move on." Time will now start to replenish what you have depleted, and the team will heal. Then wound them no more.

The Blue Bottle Tree

Even today around my home in the low country of South Carolina, having a blue bottle tree in the yard is a well-kept modernity of a generations-old Gullah/Geechee practice. The trees are usually structures of metal branches welded or wired together, with blue glass bottles stuck over the ends of the branches. The concept is they capture evil 'haints' (spirits) from making their way into one's home. The haints are lured inside the bottle by light reflected thru the blue bottle at sundown and subsequently trapped inside. Then once the sun rises the haints are vaporized by the sun's light.

One of my old supervisors had a blue bottle just outside of her office. I never really thought much about it, in fact as time went by I was so desensitized to it that I didn't even notice its existence. One evening as we were in her office discussing solution options to a pressing issue, and when we decided that we had chosen our best course of action we pronounced the work day over and planned to walk to the parking lot together. As she left her office she picked up the bottle and ritually put something invisible inside it. Seeing my concern for her odd behavior she told me that she always dropped her workplace worries and pressures in the bottle so they would not go home with her, then she would dump them back out in the morning. They couldn't escape from the 'special' cobalt blue bottle so they would faithfully wait for her return.

Whether your workplace pressures evaporate in the sun, or simply wait for you to pick them back up when you return, take the time to deliberately 'capture' the stresses that threaten to keep our lives out of balance once we close shop for the day. Just maybe a blue bottle ritual will suit you as well.

"False commitment, is theft in plain view of the victim." - My father, Cleave Hagler, Cherokee / Choctaw Author and Sage

I present to you, the passive-aggressive stakeholder. Sneaky in their approach, publicly supportive and privately destructive. As one of my colleagues recently put it... "passive-aggressives instantly breathe life into an initiative with their strident support and then kill it slowly with a thousand cuts of veto."

Even after raising their voice in agreement, when the meeting is adjourned they will inevitably send out an e-mail shooting down the idea with a strategically developed "CC" distribution list attached. If you have a call to action that is distributed electronically they will likely just pocket-veto the project by withholding their response until it is too late for preemptive course correction, forcing you to start over.

Does that sound familiar? Passive-aggressive stakeholders are disruptive to the healthy course of challenging the status quo and assembling our best process improvements with any hope of exploiting the benefit of speed-to-market.

Here is how to deal with the passive-aggressive stakeholder.

Recognize the passive-aggressive stakeholder for who they are.

Constrict membership to your tribe. Once the tribe is formed take an extra step to further constrict the group around those who are most likely to challenge the status quo and least likely to settle for anything short of an excellent result.

Mitigate your risks. You still might not catch the potential practitioner of passive-aggression early enough and they knit themselves into the fabric of a team of stakeholders. From the launch of your campaign stay focused and clear in communication. Document decisions and agreements with written follow-up to all stakeholders in an "as I remember it" or "to memorialize our agreement" memo or e-mail. You can certainly give space for a reply including any realty-check edits just to take advantage of the better memory of salient point from the collective group, but you want to keep the group on the same page from the beginning. This is not to be presented as a CYA tactic, but it will work to keep the group directionally motivation when everyone is operating from a consistent understanding.

If an implementation or post-implementation deliverable is not fully met, the same people that demonstrate passive-aggressive traits present a risk of derailing the initiative ex-post-facto.

- Take immediate ownership of the failure
- Do not make excuses
- Lastly, consult a broader group as to what they believe the contributing factors to the performance gap to be, as well as what they see as important corrective actions. This will take the 'Pied Piper' role away from any single dissenter.

"Don't let the Boo Hag ride yah." - Gullah Saying

Gullah had a folk tale about the Boo Hag, a supernatural entity that would ride you like a horse at night while you slept. Legend says that if you've had a restless night of sleep that it was most likely due to a visit from the Boo Hag.

As a leader you take action, do, accomplish, decide, direct, develop, and achieve. And you know as well as I do, that you all too often resist rest. However, rest is key to effectiveness and productivity. Integrate regular rest into your life you will see positive results demonstrated as increased stamina and clarity of mind and you will move decisively through the epochs along your continuum of leadership legacy.

Prioritize rest:

- Invest in
  - family
  - recreation
  - relationships
  - spirituality
  - sleep, snooze, nap, power down
- Keep the Sabbath... aka – take a real day off, boss!
- Balance
- Meditate
- Journal

It is better to have less thunder in the mouth and more lightning in the hand. - Apache

Speak softly and carry a big stick, was the foreign policy of President Theodore Roosevelt. When leaders practice speaking softly it is in the demonstration of honesty, integrity, transparency, compassion, humility, and maturity.

Bring out the big sticks – the lightning that leaders have in abundance, and we get action beyond words...

Leadership Lightening:

- Mentorship
- Challenge the status quo
- Broad, powerful, compelling communication
- Inspiration/motivation
- Relationship builder
- Disrupt
- Collaborate and nurtures teamwork
- Strategy
- Expertise
- Empowerment
- Analysis
- Prospective
- Innovation
- Results – deliver more than promised
- Goals
- Metrics
- Initiative
- Coalesces stakeholders

- Sells
- Leads and champions change
- Transformation
- Empowerment (yes, it's worth saying twice)

Leaders never talk the big show, if they got the big GO!

"Before eating, always take time to thank the food." - Arapaho

Do you appreciate the work? 'Saying grace' for a good day of work ahead of you is very similar to saying grace over a meal that has been set before you.

When I kick off a team meeting I like to start with a team reflection to center us and create a sense of place and presence. In the course of a reflection, I like to state appreciation for the work. "I am glad this is our work... I am thankful that we are entrusted to do it well... and I am so appreciative that we are commissioned to this service together."

Take time to thank the work.

"If we wonder often, the gift of knowledge will come." - Arapaho

GO!

- To the gemba.
- To the client.
- To the meeting.
- To the manufacturer, the distributor, the shipper.
- To the bank.
- To the retreat.
- To the extreme.
- To the doctor.
- To the sales meeting, the marketing and field planning meeting, the divisional meeting.
- To the line.
- To the branch.
- To the team.
- To the place of learning.
- To work.
- Home.

Be gone, be educated, wonder as you wander, and be back soon to teach what you have learned.

"Lie down with dogs, get up with fleas." –
Blackfoot Axiom

Our peers and colleagues can be the source of valuable counsel and support... They can also have fleas. Those little toxic behaviors that may be slight and move in near silence, but will bite you and welt up in workplace disengagement, suspicion, and you being painted with the same negative broad-brush as your destructive peers. To associate yourself with peers who demonstrate noxious collegial traits, you not only degrade your leadership and legacy, but your reputation-by-association will be distracting and productivity-draining for your team.

Watch out for these potential flea-ridden peer traits.

drama

gossip

sabotage

emotional escalation and immaturity

anxiety

aggressiveness

narcissism

passivity

lack of credibility

lack of organization

change averse

"There is nothing as eloquent as a rattlesnake's tail." - Navajo Proverb

As leaders, we are required to coalesce a meaningful portfolio of metrics to check the pulse of our operations. Libraries of books are written on developing - metrics, fortunes in consulting fees are billed to identify - metrics, applications installed and maintained to collect and warehouse data for-metrics, and decision support teams are employed to determine, extract, and report - metrics. And they are just that important.

But ya wanna know the secret sauce? Ya wanna know what metrics will let you hear the rattlesnake's tail and warn you of danger ahead for your success and your team's success? Well, here it is... Above all the other disciplinary-driven pulse metrics, monitor these three things, and IF performance sustains in decline – be ready to meet your replacement, the crew that will outplace or outsource your team, and say hello to organizational irrelevance and goodbye to being a strategic differentiator for your company. *

1. Opportunities created
2. Calls made on accounts
3. Conversions/closings

Sound like sales? It is sales... On a very primal level leadership is sales, often internal, but sales none the less. You know you have converted (or closed) the internal sale when you get the nod to develop the new program or launch the new cost reduction campaign, or highlight the competency of your team by expanding their influence or role in the company.

To convert the call, follow the four Ps... Professionalism, Practicality, Proof, and Perspective (references).

Prepare to speak competently and in a compelling way about benefits, ROI, payback, TCO, NPV, hurdle rate, and IRR.

If you have created fewer opportunities this quarter than last quarter... hear that rattle?

If you made fewer calls about supporting a new or existing opportunity... now do you hear it?

If you are sustaining a declining number of team ideations into enterprise strategy – you may feel the bite before hearing the rattle.

Those my friend – are metrics to live by.

* Is that overly-dramatic? Sorry. My bad.

"A person with many children has as many homes." - Lakota Sioux Saying

A leader's "children?"

> Networks
>
> Associations
>
> Affiliations
>
> Peers
>
> Direct reports
>
> Ideas
>
> Campaigns
>
> SKAs
>
> Colleagues
>
> Friends
>
> Cohorts

You never know when you need a home, or will be approached by those in need of one.

"Threat foreknown is threat outwitted."
- Cheyenne Proverb

Vividly envision your team being madly successful!

Most good leaders readily visualize reward. The great leaders also anticipate the steeplechase hurdles that pop up in the course of the race. The challenges, wet blankets, and unforeseen conditions that are set in potential to pop up out of nowhere – at key times – and arrest our uninhibited achievement. Give the team space to inculcate competent proactive planning for how these tests are dealt with and you have some contingency to overcome trials that might have blindsided you down the road.

"A rocky field does not need your prayer; it needs your sweat, and a pick ax." - Contemporary Navajo Truism

To influence people, you need to be able to present your case effectively. At times this calls for painting a portrait of the future with the bright colors of an exciting and captivating vision. But when the presentation is based on turning around a process, product, or team that is off track or out-of-spec, you will need to speak with utility. A compelling but practical back-to-spec model that is simple to understand and navigate, time sensitive with current benchmarks and datum, with flexibility relative to detail insights and perspectives with a competent risk analysis and basic metrics.

"A person who is pretending to be asleep cannot be awakened." - Contemporary Navajo Truism

Dormancy is a period in an organism's life cycle when growth, development, and physical activity are temporarily halted. This minimizes metabolic activity and therefore helps an organism to conserve energy. Have you ever experienced a team in a state of dormancy? Have you seen them at a time when they seem to work on autopilot, accomplishing only the minimum requirement to keep the department functional, but not engaging any stretch goals, and certainly not taking any risks to make an outstanding contribution?

John McCarthy, Assistant Professor of Human Resource Studies, ILR School, Cornell University wrote in his insightful online CAHRS ReaserchLink white paper "Dormant Ties: Out of Sight, But Not Out of Mind"* that while troubling this behavior is neither good or bad, and through study results he shows that the demonstration of dormancy exhibited in team members is likely their conservation of organizational energy in deference to a past (dormant) relationship with the organization, supplanting a current relationship they perceive as unfavorable. Even after years of no contact, the goodwill and knowledge that remain from a relationship may cause these dormant ties to spring to mind for people.

As a leader in this situation, you will need to depend on ongoing investment in trust-building practices. Building a new base of trust will likely provide immediate returns, and create fertile ground for extended yields, even after current colleagues move elsewhere in the organization -thus providing new branches upon which your leadership legacy will grow.

To be more proactive, invest as well in an awareness of the past relationships of the individual contributors on your team as well as their current network.

There is another interesting proactive, deliberate approach that few leaders that I have observed take, and it is supported in Professor McCarthy's white paper. Try actively encouraging your team to reconnect with past organizational relationships. Since team member dormancy is only deleterious if the causal conditions are ignored, and it can result in a helpful connectedness and commitment to the organization when needed, our teams will likely benefit from thoughtful, safe, competent management of the condition.

*

http://digitalcommons.ilr.cornell.edu/cgi/viewcontent.cgi?articl
e=1038&context=cahrs_researchlink

Treasure youth, trust old age, have confidence in experience." – Modernized Pueblo Truism

As a leader and as a parent I am fascinated by the population group we call "millennials." My daughter is a member of this channel of society, as have been numerous colleagues I have worked with. While as accomplished and readily mentored as any other developing leader that I have met, they have some specific attributes that are helpful to be aware of.

For instance, they suffer from an advanced stage case of FOMO - the fear of missing out... This interesting social phobia keeps them so intent on meaningful experience trumping all things that a growing economy nearly $1.3 billion deep has sprung up directed at getting millennials to open their wallets to 'experiences' versus accumulating more 'things' as predeceasing generations have done.

This is also true at work. When you lead a team infused with millennials a focus on providing experiential opportunities may help energize their connectedness to the organization and their engagement with the individual contributors on the team, as well as your customers. Besides providing an interesting experience to build upon, help them with a context to be social and broadcast their experiences across contemporary media. Encourage them to contribute to a team Facebook page or Twitter account, or Snapchat from a tradeshow booth – team Skype and Slack lists may be more immediate mediums to communicate about live events on a broad scale.

Don't be surprised when the excitement of sharing meaningful live experiences starts to infect people across generational lines and your team begins to further diversify and grow with a hunger for more great opportunities and experiences.

"Make my enemy brave and strong, so that if defeated, I will not be ashamed." - Plains Nations Proverb (Likely attributable to Blackfoot)

I challenge...

> The status quo, where it is most entrenched.
>
> The market leading competitor.
>
> The most experienced candidate when I am applying for a position.
>
> The lowest handicap golfer.
>
> The long-shot bet.
>
> The hardest worker (so I can work harder).
>
> The better funded, better-sponsored project (so my project gets the better status, better organizational attention, and delivers better results).
>
> The biggest, the hairiest, the most audacious goal (so I can achieve beyond it).

Challenge the best, and even if you only achieve inside the top 20th percentile, you are still ahead of 80% of the field.

And if you do pin the champ to the mat, you get a cool belt!

"A people without a history is like the wind over buffalo grass." – Traditional indigenous proverb found attributed to Lakota, Sioux, and Navaho peoples.

A team benefits from a palpable sense of heritage. It roots them when they would otherwise be tossed around on the winds of change – like buffalo grass being tossed about by persistent prairie breezes.

As a leader keep the team aware of inherited traditions, monuments, objects, and culture, as well as the meanings, and behaviors that we draw from them. Be sure your team heritage is safely subject to active team reflection, debate, and discussion. What do we remember? What about our heritage do we enjoy or regret? What have we learned from it?

Challenge the team in the intellectual construct that <u>today</u> they are building the heritage moments for those that come this way after them. What is important for future team members to remember about us?

"The moon is not shamed by the barking of dogs."
– Contemporary ascription to Pueblo Nation.

I learned this from a Facebook meme... "Haters gonna hate!"
You are making change happen, challenging processes and held
beliefs that are holding your team and the organization back
from excellence... You are making an omelet and eggs are going
to get broken. When your team is found having to weather
public criticism, focus here:

- Resist the temptation to "fire back"
- Don't amplify the criticism by projecting your own
  insecurities onto it
- Understand where the criticism is coming from
- Be self-aware (is there any truth in the criticism that you
  need to own?)
- Meet destructive criticism head on in constructive ways

It's your responsibility to make sure the team gets the message
in times when purposeless negativity has been aimed at them, it
is just that – purposeless – and while you will approach the
purveyor of pointless disparagement on their behalf, they
shouldn't worry about it... just move on and keep doing the
great work they have been doing.

"It takes a thousand voices to tell a single story." - Native American Proverb, Tribe Unknown

When you develop a diverse workforce, and a diverse supplier portfolio, you contribute to:

> ... economic growth and greater market share through a more effective internal barometer of the broader marketplace.

> ... a better-qualified team, by hiring from a broader spectrum of the best and brightest.

> ... avoiding excessive employee turnover costs.

> ... a more peculiarly creative and innovative contingent of solutions architects helping you solve problems and bring products to market.

> ... keeping pace with the national landscape of changing business demographics.

> ... benefitting from a fast-growing, momentum-delivering, channel of entrepreneurism.

> ... harnessing the talents of all the community to better compete in the globalized economy.

By 2050, the story of the United States will be one told by the thousand voices, as there will likely be no racial or ethnic majority. It simply makes sense to be cognizant of the benefits of a competent, talented, diverse workplace to represent all that is best from these changing demographics.

"Even today's moon in better light than yesterday's sun." - Cherokee proverb, modernized by Will Rogers as "Don't let yesterday use up too much of today."

When good leaders are drug down by the weight of past mistakes or regret, it hurts me on a very personal level. I have had to face pointing myself toward a new avenue of success when circumstances from my past are trying to drag me down and my future is placed into uncertainty. The lonely pondering of how to turn a failing business opportunity around is a wrestling match with paralysis as we struggle to take the next necessary actions. There are lessons I have learned from my time in the barrel.

If you over-analyze it, you won't move on. It just is what it is... Now get moving.

The fear of the unknown is the path to paralysis. Just decide on the path and go! Your bias at this point is for action. Your decision making is directionally correct and you can adjust course as you move forward.

Timelines are immediately important. Set them and hold yourself accountable to them. You can reassess while in motion, but these will be the goals that you will one day consider the "turning point" in your recovery.

The hardest thing you will face now is asking for help and support so you don't walk this treacherous path alone. Needing support (and you do need it) does not make you weak. It shows that you are emotionally mature and you're are strong enough, resourceful enough, and self-aware enough to reach out to someone who can make a big difference for you and the team(s) you lead.

"A true chief gives, and does not take."
– Mohawk Proverb

There are things that truly awful leaders regularly steal from their team...

Their freedom - when micro-managed...

Goals – achievement and competition are fun – at least more engaging than work-work-work.

Purpose

Mission

Worth (biggest – fastest – quickest – BEST)

Expectations - autonomy disappears when there is no base of expectation for the team to make even rudimentary decisions for themselves.

Consistency

Connection

Heritage

Input

Honesty - when a team is made implicit in a leader's 'fib and spin'.

Integrity

Respect

Voice

Community

Credit and recognition

Celebration

Pride

And money. Thwarting your team's better chances of success hampers their earning potential and keeps them from earning incremental performance bonuses and compensation increases.

"The bird who has eaten cannot fly with the bird that is hungry." – Omaha People Tribal Saying

Stay hungry, stay foolish, start something big – or small – for heaven's sake start something! Value each and every one of your motivations no matter how material they seem at this moment.

I know authors, leaders, physicians, nurses, mothers, fathers, senators, soldiers, administrators, athletes, each one an ACHIEVER. And none of them were any of those things when they set out 'to become'... So here and now - while you are hungry – fly higher faster and with more purpose than the satiated birds who are done foraging and hunting and are not in lumbering, satisfied flight.

Come see ein like come stay. (example: ["Come see"] Dating isn't the same as ["come stay"] a life-long commitment.) – Gullah Truism

Over time I have developed a personal axiom for testing ideas as "pilot locally, and implement to scale." A pilot test will help confirm if an idea is viable in a practical context, and if your team is ready for full-scale implementation. A localized pilot will gauge your target population's reaction to the program. Pilots help you make better decisions about resource allocation and measuring the success of a program.

Without running effective local pilots your team risks micro-implementations that drive up operating variability and waste resources. Test projects at scale and you will be in for never-ending measurement and radically fluctuating indicators – you will never get out of implementation testing and transition the program to an operating state.

Also without effective pilot programs, we may 'improve' processes that we should have never been doing in the first place. Set your toll gates by reciting the ballad of the industrial engineer...

> Standardize the necessary,
>
> Centralize the standardized,
>
> Simplify the standardized,
>
> Automate the simplified.

Now that you 'come see' - you are ready for 'come stay!'

"If fish de a river bottom and tell yu de alligator have gum boil believe him." (Listen to the voice of experience) - Gullah Traditional Saying

Please consider the following chart.

If you listen to advice, only with the intent to reply, and not with the intent to understand... Welcome to the little circle.

Magic happens here

Your comfort zone is here

If you receive advice and consider it valid, but take no action, wait quietly in the little circle, and think deeply about the excuses you are undoubtedly conjuring at this very minute.

Either way, wait there and the alligator will be along shortly, don't worry, he will know what to do.

If, however; you have been prudently analyzing your advisories, and you know the advice that has the ring of experiential truth, it makes sense to you... AND YOU EMBRACE IT – then get in that big circle... you are going to make magic happen!

"Don't let the windows of your home be so small that the light of the sun cannot enter your rooms."
- Native Alaskan Wisdom

George Bernard Shaw said, "Those who cannot change their minds cannot change anything."

Dogmatic leadership is a common pathology among those who value themselves as high-achievers. While their more open-minded colleagues are concerned with sustaining long-term gains of a strong and engaged workplace community, the dogmatic leader will close their mind to input since that will challenge the authority of their command and control decision structure.

Consider these four profiles of leadership relative to receptiveness to input, new ideas, or augmenting opinion.

> The over-reliant... Easily influenced by others, low self-worth regarding your own ideas.

> The rejecter... Only your opinion has value and not having a comprehensive plan or all the answers is a sign of weakness that you are not willing to demonstrate.

> The open-minded... You strike a balance, you value your own opinion and you know the answer is better with diverse input, so you seek out the opinions of others.

> The best-and-final... You are clearly open-minded, and you have a precise understanding of the connectedness of all the datum you are using to flesh out your idea. Once you inculcate all of the augmenting opinions and input, you take one more refining pass at modeling a

best-case, move-forward position from the best
performing scenario.

"If you are going to walk on thin ice, you might as well dance." - Native Alaskan Truism

The condition makes success critical. No changing the timeline, no time to 'phase in' a plan with sustainable gains. Maybe it was thrust upon you by circumstance outside of your control, or perhaps it is your own designed disruption. The conservative approach is expected and even preferred by those who will take your initiative's poll position and move their team ahead of yours in terms of organizational focus and support. Don't do what is expected, don't give them the satisfaction. Do the unexpected...

Go for broke

Hail Mary

All-or-nothing

Stop fumbling around

Be gutsy

Be audacious

Go for the win

Swing for the fences

Pull out all the stops

Balls to the wall

DANCE!

"May your charity increase as much as your wealth." – Contemporary Native Alaskan Proverb

It's almost as if the universe is making sure that you can't get this one wrong. In fact, it seems that you can't really accumulate things that you are not willing to give away. Maybe it's because we don't mentally track giving away things that we don't place a higher value on in the first place. I am not certain what makes it work, but it does work – and it works to build better leaders, stronger communities, and a better quality of life.

Have you increased in knowledge or skill? Teach it!

Are you paid more? Find a cause and donate to it!

Did your increased understanding guide you to discover a business process that is simply the right thing to do? Do it! Figure out how to make it pay later!

Did the mental light bulb come on and you now see that the right thing to do falls outside of the accepted rationality of your industry? Challenge the logic of your industry!

Did you get a new car? Drive a shift in an office carpool!

Become proficient at giving, and your wealth (however you define it) becomes a tide that raises all ships.

"The caribou feeds the wolf, but it is the wolf who keeps the caribou strong." - Inuit Proverb

Friedrich Nietzche said it as "... that which does not kill us, makes us stronger." Interesting isn't it? The thought that we should be thankful for our tribulations and threats since they keep our acuity high, and our skills sharp.

Be thankful for how that period of time that you were out of work sharpened your focus on the industry and forced you to fix skills gaps in your experience.

Be thankful for organizational politics since it helps you develop the executive maturity to rise above it and be a better Vice President for your region.

Missed growth target for a quarter... Delivering a compelling back-to-plan strategy to stockholders makes you are a stronger Chief Executive.

Unfavorable expense trends in your area of responsibility... Intensive value engineering makes you a stronger manager and develops new lines of benefit that accrete to directly to incremental revenue.

Late to work – better future commuter.

Fender bender – better driver.

Loss for words in a meeting – better impromptu public speaker.

Yes, I am thankful for my struggles, the day will come when I need (once again) to outrun the wolf.

"Yesterday is ashes; tomorrow wood. Only today does the fire burn brightly." – Contemporary Native Alaskan Aphorism

You are good at so many things... so... accomplished. How is your performance in these key areas?

Moment

Less

Deliberate

One thing at a time

Savor

Hang a "back in five" sign and power down – power nap – eat a power bar

Breathe

Flow

Balance

TOSS (Take On Simple Stuff) good way to meditate

Meditate

Accept

Engage

Don't fret the future

Slow – savor food – savor life

Accomplish even more... Don't just do something... Sit there!

Let us put our minds together and see what life we can make for our children." - Sitting Bull

How we engage with the world carries over to the life approach of children who observe us. If you espouse that living is an exhausting series of accelerating challenges, missed targets, bad luck, and unmanageable objectives, it should come as no surprise when that is how these cute little attitude sponges begin to view their life and opportunities as well.

A child who sees life as great, positive, hopeful, wonderful, full of possibilities and waiting to be explored; likely experienced an influential adult that felt the same way.

We are often responsible for so much more than we are directly accountable for in terms of the job description or budget performance. As a leader keep in mind that as the individual contributors on your team go home to their families, the manner that you influence them will accrete to their children.

Set the stage for generations of success by being the boss that your direct reports will be proud of when their kids emulate your influence… Yes, it's a matter of "when," not "if."

"It is not necessary for eagles to be crows." - Sitting Bull

At times corporate growth plans are more focused on merger and acquisition than they are about organic marketplace growth and the development of new product and service offerings. Merging multiple operating teams is a distinct competency that requires specific skill and focus.

Leading cultural integration requires defining the differences that matter so a new team can move on to the important work of coalescing the future-state culture that will welcome all the contributors to the new integrated team and contribute in meaningful ways to the incremental future value of the new enterprise.

What differences matter?

Management styles.

Side-by-side comparisons of how people do similar jobs. (Videos and process flow charts – from the "gemba")

Compare the RACI chart (who is "Responsible, "Accountable, "Consulted" and "Informed) for how decisions are made and implemented.

Acceptable behaviors.

Prevalent attitudes.

Current priorities.

Practices of equity.

Rituals.

Celebrations.

Heritage.

"What is life?

It is the flash of a firefly in the night.

It is the breath of a buffalo in the wintertime.

It is the little shadow which runs across the grass

and loses itself in the sunset."

~ Native American Proverb

When your job starts taking over your life...

> Book family time in your schedule.

> If you are run-down, rest for a day.

> If something hurts, go to the doctor.

> Simple leadership life-hack... Don't work on airplanes. Personally, I can always tell when someone was working on a flight, their work is sub-par and unacceptable... I see it with everyone, every time. Why do perfectly awful work that you will have to apologize for and likely re-do anyway? Enjoy the flight. Read a book, watch a movie.

> Put sacred buffer time between meetings on your schedule. Run from meeting to meeting and you get behind, get a reputation for tardiness, and insult people by making them wait for you.

> Get physical: Exercise during the day, park in the far spaces in the back parking lot, take the stairs.

Pick and choose, say no, be self-aware enough to know what is important.

Give up – surrender - move on to something more productive – enough is enough – don't keep throwing pearls before swine.

"Old age is not as honorable as death, but most people want it." - Native American Proverb, Likely Attributable to the Crow Nation

I read that the Mediterranean diet will help me prevent heart disease... That 30 minutes of exercise every day has the same level of health benefit as quitting smoking does... By the way, we have all heard about the benefits of being a non-smoker. I also just recently skimmed through an article about how a daily walk can add seven years to my life.

Over time, I have also heard about how smoking, a sedentary lifestyle, overwork, stress, overeating, obesity, worry, fighting, promiscuity, drinking, and of course smoking will all shave years OFF of my life.

I don't want to give the impression that I am gullible about blindly following health fads, but doesn't it make sense that some behaviors contribute favorably to our lifespan and some go the other way?

Ya gotta **'DO'** all of these things, my friends... why stack the deck against yourself?

"Wolf is always out there waiting, and wolf is always hungry." - Navajo Proverb

The angry wolf and the kind wolf – both hungry – both know you will feed one and not the other – both represent choices that only I can make – choices that influence, affect, directionally inspire so many important people in my life.

I cherish being in a position to lead and influence people to achieve great things and take advantage of substantial opportunities in their lives. It's personally rewarding and it's emotionally addictive.

Since this is my calling and my priority, I have decided to feed only the wolf that is called Joy, Peace, Love, Hope, Serenity, Humility, Kindness, Benevolence, Empathy, Generosity, Truth, Compassion, and Faith... These are the things that I want my team to experience at work. These are the things that I want their families to know me by. These are the things that my wife will depend on me for, and my daughter will emulate from my example.

Choose well – lead with maturity and strength.

Blessings

Tim

Timothy Hagler is an experienced life sciences supply chain leader, with an ever-accelerating interest in earnestly connecting stakeholders with creative ideas to meet new economic realities for healthcare providers. Tim has enjoyed an excellent track record of achievement and advancement earned through demonstrated contribution to bottom-line results, employing strong solutions architecture, analytic and financial skills in challenging, multi-client environments. Tim and his lovely wife Kandy enjoy spending time at the beach in South Carolina. Tim's hobbies include photography, American folk music, and writing about himself in the third person.

In his 1947 Western novel 'Blood Brother', Elliott Arnold wrote this text inspired by a traditional (attributed Apache) blessing. Even though assumptions about the original attribution being of native inspiration is clouded in ambiguity, the sentiment is quite beautiful, well versed by Mr. Arnold, and it is my wish for you.

May the sun bring you

new energy by day,

may the moon softly restore

you by night,

may the rain wash away

your worries,

may the breeze blow new

strength into your being,

may you walk gently through

the world and know it's

beauty all the days

of your life.

www.ingramcontent.com/pod-product-compliance
Lightning Source LLC
Chambersburg PA
CBHW021413170526
45164CB00002B/634